trotman

BERYL DIXON

Sport & Fitness

UNCOVERED

Sport and Fitness Uncovered
This first edition published in 2004 by Trotman and Company Ltd
2 The Green, Richmond, Surrey TW9 1PL

© Trotman and Company Limited 2004

Editorial and Publishing Team

Author Beryl Dixon
Editorial Mina Patria, Editorial Director; Rachel Lockhart,
Commissioning Editor; Anya Wilson, Editor;
Bianca Knights, Assistant Editor
Production Ken Ruskin, Head of Pre-press and Production
Sales and Marketing Tom Lee, Commercial Director;
Deborah Jones, Head of Sales and Marketing
Managing Director Toby Trotman

Designed by XAB

British Library Cataloguing in Publication Data
A catalogue record for this book is available
from the British Library

ISBN 0 85660 964 1

Typeset by Palimpsest Book Production Limited,
Polmont, Stirlingshire

Printed and bound in Great Britain by Cromwell Press,
Trowbridge, Wiltshire

CONTENTS

About the Author

Beryl Dixon is an experienced careers adviser who has worked for different local education authorities and in a tertiary college where she helped students of all ages with their decisions on both higher education and employment. She has also worked for the Ministry of Defence and the Department for Education and Skills, visiting schools in Brussels, Luxembourg, Cyprus and Hong Kong to provide careers advice to the children of expatriate service personnel and government officials.

She now concentrates on careers writing and is the author of several books, including *What can I do with an Arts Degree?*, *What can I do with a Social Sciences Degree?*, *How to Choose your Postgraduate Course* (Trotman Publishing), *Jobs and Careers after A Level and other Advanced Qualifications* and *Decisions at 16 Plus* (Lifetime Careers Publishing). She also writes for a number of publications, including *YouCan*, UCAS' magazine for A-level students and *Careerscope*, the magazine of the Independent Schools' Careers Organisation.

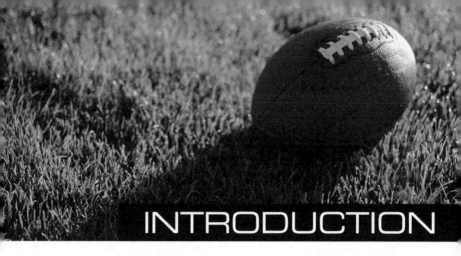

INTRODUCTION

Any idea how many events take place at an Olympic Games?
Athens 2004 hosted 296 individual events with 11,000 competitors.
Each one with a coach and network of support staff to help them
attain peak fitness.

Don't worry. You do not have to be an Olympic athlete to enjoy a
career in sport and fitness! The whole industry is booming with
thousands of gyms, personal trainers and a whole host of new
classes regularly coming onto the scene.

WHY READ THIS BOOK?

Because you have started to think about careers. It's never too
early to do so. There are dozens of jobs out there. Some would be
right for you; some wouldn't. Some you will be qualified to do;
others you won't. That said, you still have a pretty wide choice –
and you want to get it right. So by starting here you are beginning
your research into which job or jobs are likely to be best for you.
You will be able to work out which careers fit best with your:

● personality

● interests

● skills

● values.

WHY THINK OF A CAREER IN SPORT AND FITNESS?

'Because I enjoy it', you'll probably say. 'And because I can be paid to spend all day doing something I enjoy.' Right. These are two very good reasons. A third is that these are areas that offer plenty of jobs. Everywhere you look there are gyms, health clubs, recreation and leisure centres – many privately owned, some attached to hotels, some owned by local authorities (although these are usually managed by commercial firms). Then there is the fact that you will benefit personally. You will be fit and healthy yourself!

WHY ARE THERE SO MANY JOBS?

- Because fitness is a growing industry. There are about 1,000 council leisure centres, plus 4,500 fitness centres and 500 clubs in offices and factories.

- People are spending more time on leisure activities and fitness. The average working week in Britain is 37.5 hours. Take out the time spent travelling to and from work and in doing household chores and other necessary stuff, and there's quite a lot of time left for leisure. If you opt for a career in sport and fitness you can be involved in your work in something that other people pay to do. BUT it will be work! Don't forget that.

- People of all ages and income levels are able to spend time and/or money on health and fitness. People who have been able to take early retirement take up golf, swimming or rambling, or take out membership of a health club. Sue Hornibrook (see page 26), who works in a private health club, refers to off-peak membership taken out by older people who are able to come in at quiet times – and take part in any of dozens of classes. Unemployed people and students also benefit from concessions at off-peak times. Some high earners, celebs and stressed professionals see the benefits of staying fit and healthy. People like Madonna and the Prime Minister are widely rumoured to employ personal trainers. Some well-off clients have their own home gyms and employ trainers who come to them. Christianne Wolff (see page 33) has famous people among her clients.

Some people enjoy being active. Others are encouraged or bullied into it. They read newspaper articles promoting healthy lifestyles or are advised to take up some form of physical activity by their doctor. (Some doctors recommend swimming or supervised gym workouts to patients with conditions ranging from heart disease to obesity.)

Not too high a risk of unemployment then. But what about pay? True, you could earn your living doing something that you enjoy (a hopeless dream for many people chained to the office or the factory floor) but this is not the highest-paid area of work. We can't all be David Beckham or Venus Williams. It is difficult to make a living in professional sport, in fact – and only a very few very highly paid individuals make it to the top. Most professional sportsmen/women also have other jobs to support themselves. But there are literally dozens of other jobs in sport and fitness: some pay well, others don't. (Employers can get away with paying less to enthusiasts and they sometimes rely on job satisfaction being more important than loads of cash.)

This book, like others in the series, will give you the low-down on these jobs. You will find job descriptions, factual information on training, prospects and likely earnings. You'll also find out about the downsides. This book gives you the truth – warts and all. Throughout the book are case studies, so that you can read first hand what people in the sports and fitness industries say about their work. And you can read their tips and advice.

WHAT DO SOME OF THEM SAY?

MANAGER OF A LARGE LOCAL AUTHORITY LEISURE CENTRE WITH OVER 200 STAFF.
What do you like about your job?
Dealing with the public. It's never dull.
And dislike?
The bureaucracy. I spend ages on form filling and conducting risk assessments. There is a shed full of legislation on public health and safety. But it is necessary.

PE TEACHER IN A LARGE COMPREHENSIVE SCHOOL.
What do you like about your job?
Being able to indulge my own passion for sport. I teach the full range of team sports and am able to coach one I really love after school. There is a buzz in seeing my team win matches all season.
And dislike?
The problem of getting girls motivated. Sport isn't cool and there is a lot of peer pressure to conform and drop out of activities as they get higher up the school.

SELF-EMPLOYED PERSONAL FITNESS TRAINER.
What do you like about your job?
The sheer variety. I meet so many different people – and all their programmes are different. Plus I love helping people to achieve.
And dislike?
Having to do all my own paperwork and accounts.

SPORTS DEVELOPMENT OFFICER.
What do you like about your job?
I don't like it. I love it.
And dislike?
The unsocial hours are a drawback. I don't mind giving up some weekends to attend events or do some coaching, but I also have to go to a lot of evening meetings.

SPORTS PHYSIOTHERAPIST.
What do you like about your job?
The flexibility. I can work the hours I choose. And I get to meet a variety of patients.
And dislike?
Not much. But being self-employed I don't take much holiday.

YOUR TURN

So, how about becoming a personal trainer? Sports development officer? Swimming teacher? Leisure centre manager? Sports psychologist?

Careers covered in this book include those in:

● sport

● physical fitness and education

● leisure and recreation

● other areas such as health and media work.

CHAPTER 1

The truth about sport and fitness

You probably know something about the most common sports and activities – especially if you practise one or more of them. But did you know that the following all have websites?

- beach volleyball

- curling

- freestyle skiing

- luge.

Look at Yahoo's sports directory web pages for more information (http://yahoo.com/Recreation/Sports/Events).

WHY SHOULD YOU THINK ABOUT A CAREER IN SPORT AND FITNESS?

ADVICE FROM THOSE WHO KNOW

According to the Institute of Leisure and Amenity Recreation (ILAM):

- The leisure industry is huge, with a wide range of job opportunities. There are lots of 'basic'-level jobs that do not require many formal qualifications, although there are variations across the industry.

- There are also increasing numbers of openings for people with degrees.

- Many careers are genuinely open in terms of opportunities. When you've found the first job, promotion to all levels is possible. Some careers, however, do require qualifications rather than simply experience for advancement.

You could start from various entry points:

- from school at age 16/17 with some exam passes – or with no formal qualifications

- from school/college at 18/19 with A-levels or Scottish Highers

- from a college at 18/20 with a vocational qualification

- from higher education with an HND or degree

- from higher education with a postgraduate qualification

- from another career with relevant experience.

According to Sports Coach UK (the National Coaching Federation), the Government Agenda for Sport means that there will be:

- a massive increase in after-school sport and inter-school competition

- a rapid rise in the number of young people (aged under 19) involved in sports leadership and volunteering, linked to the inclusion of citizenship on the national curriculum

- an increase in sports programmes designed to tackle wider social issues (law and order, health, social exclusion).

And more jobs!

DEFINITIONS FIRST

What are the differences between sport, fitness and leisure?

Sport and fitness are part of the wider leisure industry – which is enormous. It already employs more than 750,000 people – and is growing. But that figure relates to the whole leisure sector, which includes travel and tourism as well as sport. Some tourism does include sport: there has been a growth in adventure holidays, ranging from white-water rafting to trekking. Are these leisure or tourism? No matter. They need qualified instructors. More jobs for people who want to qualify in outdoor pursuits!

So leaving out 'straight' holiday tourism, sport and fitness include all sorts of team and individual activities, from badminton to martial arts; cricket to rowing, tennis to fishing, keep fit to circuit training. Not all offer paid employment, however. You have to make the distinction between amateur and professional sport. You can't officially earn a living through athletics, for instance – unless, perhaps, by coaching. But having said that, many amateurs make a decent living from sponsoring products and giving after-dinner speeches.

SPORT

The main jobs that involve active participation in one or more sports are:

- professional player

- coach

- instructor/teacher.

Then there are openings for people who make sports activities possible. For example:

- leisure centre manager

- leisure centre assistant

- lifeguard/pool attendant

- sports development officer.

And jobs on the sidelines, in which sport is not the main skill:

- administrative, reception and sales staff in recreation and leisure centres

- sports psychologist

- physiotherapist

- sports journalist.

FASCINATING FACTS

Did you know that there are 28 sports in the summer Olympics?
Do you know what they are? (Answers at the end of this chapter.)
And did you know that an Olympic sport must be 'widely practised by men in at least 75 countries and on four continents, and by women in at least 40 countries and on three continents'?

FITNESS

Fitness is individual and personal. People have their own priorities and want workouts and routines that will help achieve them.

Jobs in the fitness industry include:

- aerobics teacher

- exercise instructor

- fitness centre/health club manager

- fitness centre/health club assistant

- personal trainer.

These jobs and many others are described in the following chapters. You will also find information on training courses. Training and qualifications are something that you will need to check out very carefully, particularly in the fitness area, where you need to look out for some rogue qualifications.

WHICH WORKING ENVIRONMENT WOULD SUIT YOU?

- Would you like to work in a small team? With colleagues who come and go on different shifts? One-to-one with a client?

- In a large centre? In one place? Moving about? On a cruise ship? Indoors? Outdoors?

Well, you're in luck. In sport and fitness you could work in any of these settings and with any combination of people. On the whole, you are not likely to work in very large organisations, other than the very big city leisure centres, which may employ as many as 200 staff. But you could work in any of the following places:

- clients' homes

- colleges

- gyms

- hospitals

- leisure and recreation centres

- newspaper offices

- outdoor pursuits centres

- schools

- shops (for sports equipment)

- sports centres

- sports fields

- stadiums

- swimming pools

- TV studios

- your own home.

And in any of the following environments:

- on golf courses
- on grass
- on horseback
- on ice

- on tracks
- on rivers
- in, on or under the sea
- underground.

HOW MUCH COULD YOU REALISTICALLY EXPECT TO EARN?

This is a notoriously difficult sector when it comes to assessing average earnings. Pay rates vary according to size of employer and location. (Pay is usually higher in London and the South East.) Overtime and unsocial hours' allowances could boost your earnings considerably. Many people working in fitness put in what many of us might regard as excessively long hours in overtime (but so does a City banker) – and therefore earn much more than any average figures quoted. They would say that they do not regard taking evening keep fit, dance, aerobics or circuit training sessions as work. They enjoy doing it. What do you think?

As a rough guide, however:
Leisure centre assistants may either be paid hourly or receive an annual salary. Whichever way it is calculated they are likely to earn from £8,000 to £14,000 per year. This is the basic salary for a working week of about 37 hours.

Leisure centre managers usually earn somewhere between £20,000 and £25,000 a year. Managers of the largest centres earn more – in the region of £35,000 plus company car.

Many centre assistants and supervisors or junior managers raise their earnings by working evening and weekend shifts for additional payment, and by running classes at the centre in activities that they are qualified to teach.

Sports coaches – well, for a start there are very few full-time paid positions. Most of those enthusiastic souls who give up their time to coach pupils after school or junior teams on Saturdays are volunteers doing it for sheer pleasure. Some coaches do work professionally (often combining this work with another job) and can expect to earn around £20 an hour. At the very top of the profession salaries of £40,000 are on offer – and the really top-drawer coaches earn more.

Personal trainers are either paid as leisure centre assistants or supervisors, or are self-employed. If you look at the website of the National Register of Personal Trainers (www.nrpt.co.uk) you will see ads from trainers, quoting their range of expertise and their fee levels. Most charge £25–£30 per hour. In the centre of well-heeled areas – Knightsbridge and Chelsea in London, and cities like Leeds and Manchester – some charge over £60. Out of this must come the cost of (and time taken) travelling to visit clients or fees for booking space and equipment in a gym.

Professional players – the sky's the limit here. Or it is for the successful and famous. The B-list have to support themselves through other jobs.

Teachers in state schools are paid on salary scales ranging from £18,105 (£21,522 in inner London) to £26,460 (£30,000 in inner London). That's if they do not get promoted. Taking on more responsibilities means they can earn up to £39,093 in inner London and £33,150 outside London. Heads of large schools can get up to £88,155 (£94,098 in inner London). But then, they are not teaching sport!

The real baddies in the payment stakes are some equestrian centres. Many really do rely on enthusiasm from their staff and pay pathetically low salaries when you take into account all the hours riding instructors work. (They also have to look after the horses when work is over.) They do have to be paid the minimum wage, of course, but it's not uncommon for staff, especially trainees, to work 60 hours a week. Needless to say, many of them wouldn't consider doing anything else. Once again, money isn't everything. Qualified instructors can earn from £17,000 to £23,000, however, and those with the highest qualifications, which means passing lots of exams and becoming a fellow of the British Horse Society, can demand up to £35,000.

SOME GENUINE JOB ADS

These all appeared in leisure and sport magazines or on websites in the spring of 2004.

Team leader	West Midlands	£12,790–£13,335
Recreation assistant	South East	£13,394–£17,520
Centre supervisor	West Midlands	£13,581–£14,532
Multi-skilled coaches	North West	£14,817–£16,515
Fitness manager	South East	£15,300–£19,700
Lifeguards	London	£7.00 per hour
Part-time fitness adviser	South East	£6.94–£9.08 per hour
Assistant school sports centre manager	South East	£16,000
Sports duty manager	North West	£16,212–£18,582
Sports development officer	North West	£16,212–£20,469
Sports development officer	West Midlands	£16,944–£18,582
Community sport and leisure officer	Midlands	£16,944–£20,469
Research and marketing officer	South East	£17,006–£24,308
Swimming tuition co-ordinator	South East	£17,520–£21,583
Tennis managers	Various locations	£20,000–£32,000
Customer support manager	South East	£22,894–£27,739
Sport-specific coaches	North West	£25,000 plus
Leisure services manager	London	£31,900–£43,200
General manager, fitness company	East Anglia	£35,000–£45,000
(including target-related earnings)		

You will notice that the higher up the ladder you go, the less your job will involve active participation in sports. But this is the pattern in most jobs. Chief constables don't patrol the streets; head teachers don't work in the classroom; hotel managers don't wait in restaurants.

ARE SPORT AND FITNESS FOR YOU?

Take these quizzes to see if you might be suited to a career in sport and fitness. Answers are given below.

SPORT QUIZ

1. You have just finished a hard day's teaching in a secondary
    school. You have a pile of GCSE PE coursework to mark. You
    want to get home, have something to eat and then get on
    with it. A 14-year-old pupil comes along and asks whether
    you could spare 15 minutes to come and encourage the
    football team by discussing tactics with them.

    Do you:
    a) Say you've got too many other things to do?
    b) Arrange another time?
    c) Put your car keys away and go to the pitch?

2. You are a sports development officer at a meeting of city
    councillors. You're trying to raise funds to develop coaching
    in a poor area of the city and keep the kids off the street.
    One councillor is particularly obstructive – he thinks they
    should make their own entertainment.

    Do you:
    a) Tell him he's a dinosaur? Kids may have played quietly and
    stayed in during the war but this is 2004.
    b) Explain carefully that this a way of discouraging youth
    crime and making the area safer for the community?
    c) Sigh and look to heaven for support?

3. You coach a hockey team on Saturdays. Other things –
    holidays, invitations – keep cropping up and you can't always
    be there.

    Do you:
    a) Cancel the sessions? After all, you are giving your time free
    of charge.
    b) Resign and hand over to someone else?
    c) Make a list of which invitations are most important and find
    another coach to cover for you on a small number of
    occasions?

4. **You are a leisure centre manager. You have a friend who is a journalist.**

    Do you:
    a) Constantly feed him with stories, hoping to get the leisure centre mentioned in the paper?
    b) Decide that using friends like that is wrong?
    c) Get your photograph in his paper as often as you can?

5. **You work as a leisure centre assistant. Your supervisor suggests you attend evening classes to gain further qualifications. You can reorganise your shifts in order to go.**

    Do you:
    a) Say 'She must be joking. Do this in my own time?'
    b) Accept gratefully?
    c) Ask for help with paying the fees?

ANSWERS

1. **b)** is probably the right answer – because you are genuinely busy, although if you can manage to rejig your commitments, **c)** - going to help them now would be brilliant. a)? You shouldn't be considering this work if you are not prepared to give up time to encourage young players.

2. **b)** is correct. You will need tact and diplomacy in this line of work. Sometimes it's necessary to be very patient and make other people see your point of view. Did you answer a)? You do want the funding, don't you?

3. **c)** is correct. You can't be expected to give up everything. But what happened to commitment? Most jobs in sport involve unsocial hours – and you knew this when you took on the job.

4. **a)** is good – but why not tone it down a little? Maybe send him a list of possible stories and offer to discuss them with him. Did you answer c)? Whatever happened to teamwork? Don't other members of staff deserve their 15 minutes of fame too?

5.   Answer **c)** is OK. You are showing that you are keen to get on,
     but as you don't earn very much it's fair to make the request.
     Did you answer a)? What a way to show commitment! You do
     want to progress, don't you?

FITNESS QUIZ

1.   **You're a fitness instructor and have had a really hard day at
     the gym. Clients were grumpy and wouldn't cooperate.**

     Do you:
     a) Go home in tears?
     b) Shrug it off? You can't win' em all. Tomorrow will be
     better.
     c) Think about a nice job in an office?

2.   **You're a personal trainer. A client simply isn't putting in the
     effort.**

     Do you:
     a) Think 'Oh, well. His loss. He's paying me, after all'?
     b) Nag and bully until he gives it a bit more welly?
     c) Spend some time working out a different programme?

3.   **You have raised the finance and managed to open your own
     fitness centre. Money's still tight, though.**

     Do you:
     a) Hire staff who seem competent? You can watch them at
     work and see how well they perform.
     b) Make sure that they have approved qualifications?
     c) Recruit people who already do sessions in other clubs?
     They must be OK, after all, to be working already.

4.   **You need to bring in clients to your club.**

     Do you:
     a) Pay for newspaper advertising?
     b) Print leaflets and have them put through letter boxes?
     c) Get friends to spread the word?

5. You are a gym manager. Prospective clients ask to be shown around.

   Do you:
   a) Do it yourself?
   b) Do the tour and take a junior member of staff with you to observe?
   c) Delegate it to your deputy?

ANSWERS

1. **b)** is correct. You have to take the rough with the smooth. In any job that involves work with people – not just in this industry – there are bound to be days when you have personality clashes or problems of some kind. Answer a) or c)? Are you a wimp or what?

2. **c)** is the right answer. Personal trainers need to motivate their clients and make the sessions enjoyable. You do this by thinking that maybe your programme needs modifying, not by barking like a sergeant major.

3. Don't even think about a) or c). What would happen if there were some kind of accident, or a client makes a claim for negligence or incorrect teaching? You will need comprehensive insurance – and you won't get it if you employ unqualified staff. It's up to you to check this and not to assume that another employer has been conscientious.

4. **b)** and/or **c)**. Answer a) is ok – but pricey.

5. Any answer is correct (assuming that your deputy is competent!). Training someone else to do the job (b) would be a good move, though.

IS THE JOB RIGHT FOR YOU?

SPORT
The core skills that every sportsperson needs – player, teacher or coach – are:

- a positive attitude
- ability in one or more sports
- ability to motivate others
- communication skills
- enthusiasm
- generosity (to others on the pitch)
- leadership

- organisational skills
- patience
- self-discipline
- some knowledge of psychology
- stamina
- teamwork skills
- willingness to work unsocial hours.

'If you are interested in becoming a leisure assistant then it is essential that you are self-confident and not shy talking to people. You have to be able to make yourself heard and be assertive – particularly if you are managing a situation that could be a potential hazard to the public (e.g. if someone gets into difficulty in the pool). Being able to make quick decisions and take control of the situation is vital.'

Adam Dodd, Leisure Assistant

'Without a doubt communication skills are essential in this job. You need to be a people person as you are dealing with members of the public all day. You also need to be prepared to work long hours.'

Garry Peal, Leisure Centre Manager

FITNESS

The skills you need are:

- a positive attitude
- ability in one or more activities
- ability to be firm when necessary
- ability to motivate others
- communication skills
- diplomacy
- enthusiasm
- knowledge of health and safety
- knowledge of physiology and anatomy
- leadership
- organisational skills
- patience
- perseverance
- self-discipline
- some knowledge of psychology
- willingness to work unsocial hours.

'Skills you need in this job include organisational ability – there are a lot of different areas of work; communication skills – it is vital to keep members happy; and leadership. You have to act as a role model for staff.'

Sue Hornibrook, Assistant Health Club Manager

'The most important skills for a personal trainer are patience and communication skills. You have to be able to react to each client as an individual. Sometimes it's necessary to be assertive. At other times you have to coax. It also helps to be creative. I get bored easily myself, which helps me to see when clients are becoming bored with their programme. I then adapt it and try different activities.'

Christianne Wolff, Personal Trainer

WHAT WILL THE HOURS BE LIKE?

One – variable. Two – unsocial. (Luckily for them, few people working in sport and leisure have working hours as unsocial as those of Rob Bonnet, who presents sports reports on BBC Breakfast. He gets up at 3.45am!) You will have to work when other people are free. You can say goodbye to having every weekend free. And you will have to work some evenings. In many jobs you will work a shift or rota system. This can play havoc with your social life – but a good manager or supervisor should work out duty rotas well in advance so that staff know what shifts they have been assigned, and have the opportunity to change them with colleagues if necessary.

This is not so very different from the conditions experienced by nurses, doctors, other people employed in the health service such as paramedics and porters, people who work in hotels, police officers, firefighters and many more – even shop assistants, now that stores open seven days a week and sometimes 24/7.

HOW IMPORTANT TO YOU IS MONEY?

Have you picked up the point yet about not earning megabucks in this industry? (It's been mentioned . . . so where were you?)

FREELANCE WORK

Dream of being your own boss? Many people do. Some thrive; others can't hack it. The sport and fitness industry is full of freelance (or self-employed) people. Many of them combine several jobs in order to earn a living – working sessions here and there. Some people just want to be in sole charge of their work and work freelance, even though they could work for an employer.

Freelance opportunities in sport and fitness include working as:

● aerobics instructors

● coaches

● dance teachers

- keep-fit instructors

- personal trainers

- physiotherapists – many combine private sports injury work with NHS work

- players in some non-team sports – e.g. tennis, golf

- sports journalists

- sports photographers

- sports psychologists

- swimming teachers.

If you go down the freelance route you have to be confident that you can earn enough money, bring in enough work, manage your time, buy any equipment that you need, handle your own tax and insurance payments – and do all your own administration.

There are rewards, namely:

- you're independent

- you can choose your own hours of work

- you can decide when to go on holiday

- you can work just as hard as you choose to.

And there are downsides:

- you'll have no job security

- you will have to be constantly thinking ahead about getting more work

- you'll have to make arrangements for both professional indemnity and heath insurance. (Who pays the bills if you are off sick?)

'When I was building up my private practice, if a client wanted an appointment at three o'clock on a Saturday afternoon – they got one!'

Gill Driver, Physiotherapist

'I have to be very organised. I have to work when clients want me – which means a lot of early morning and evening work. To compensate, I no longer work at the weekend. I have to plan my work carefully and try to make appointments for clients at the gym one after another. I also arrange home visits for clients who live near to each other on the same day in order to avoid too much driving between appointments. If this is not possible I might add a charge for travelling time to my fee. It's necessary to set my own fees and do my accounts. I have to be careful not to fill the whole week with bookings. Some time has to be set aside for promoting the business and getting future work.'

Christianne Wolff, Personal Trainer

Even Christianne, who is very successful, says that there are periods when she does not earn very much – or is waiting for payment from clients to come through.

FASCINATING FACT

Olympic sports: the answers (from page 9)

- Aquatics
- Archery
- Athletics
- Hockey
- Judo
- Modern Pentathlon

- Badminton
- Baseball
- Basketball
- Boxing
- Canoeing
- Cycling
- Equestrian Events
- Fencing
- Football
- Gymnastics
- Handball
- Rowing
- Sailing
- Shooting
- Softball
- Table Tennis
- Tae Kwon Do
- Tennis
- Triathlon
- Volleyball
- Weightlifting
- Wrestling

Of course, there are many more individual sports (296, as we mentioned in the Introduction) because these are wide categories. Aquatics, for instance, is an Olympic sport with four disciplines: swimming, diving, water polo and synchronised swimming. Similarly, athletics covers a number of activities in track and field.

CHAPTER 2

What could you be in sport and fitness?

Look at these lists and see how many might interest you.

SPORTS

Athletics, Badminton, Ballooning, Basketball, Bobsleigh, Boxing, Bowling, Canoeing, Caving, Climbing, Cricket, Cycling, Diving, Fencing, Figure Skating, Football, Gliding, Golf, Gymnastics, Hang Gliding, Hockey, Ice Dance, Karate, Judo, Lacrosse, Motor Racing, Netball, Orienteering, Parachuting, Rowing, Rugby, Riding, Sailing, Scuba Diving, Shooting, Show Jumping, Snooker, Squash, Table Tennis, Tae Kwon Do, Tennis, Volleyball, Water Skiing, Windsurfing, Wrestling.

FITNESS

Aqua classes, Aerobics, Body Conditioning, Boxercise, Circuit Training, Dance, Fit Ball, Pilates, Spinning, T'ai Chi, Tap, Weights, Yoga.

No – you can't make a fortune in all of the above. Many are amateur sports. But they all offer some employment opportunities – as coaches and instructors if not as professionals.

JOBS IN SPORT AND FITNESS

COACH

Sports coaches train, advise and motivate athletes and sportsmen/women, whether amateur or professional. They provide feedback on performance, sometimes using videos to help demonstrate weaknesses and analyse potential for improvement. If working with professionals, they have to make sure that the athletes are able to cope mentally before each big event. Opportunities vary from sport to sport. Professional sports such as football and cricket have traditionally had full-time coaches, but in many other sports, including horse riding, golf and tennis, full-time positions for coaching professionals are scarce.

There are over 500,000 coaches/instructors in the United Kingdom. Only 20% of these are paid; the other 80% are volunteers. Some coach part time, and many are self-employed and work for several clubs or teams. Salaries vary according to which sports are coached and at what level – from £6 to £20 an hour.

You can read more about this career in *Careers 2005*, published by Trotman. (See Sources of information at the end of this book.)

FITNESS INSTRUCTOR

People who take exercise or fitness classes are usually known as instructors – as opposed to personal trainers, who work with individual clients. Exercise and fitness instructors might specialise in one or more – often two or three – of the following: aerobics, aqua exercise, circuit training, keep fit, resistance training, step, weight training and yoga. They must be able to carry out fitness assessments and advise clients on activities that they can undertake safely.

- The majority of employers (72 per cent) in exercise and fitness are small organisations with fewer than ten employees.

- Very few organisations employ more than 25 people.

- More women than men work in exercise and fitness.

> Information from SPRITO (National Training Organisation for
> Sport, Recreation and Allied Occupations)

GROUNDSMAN

Players expect a perfectly kept pitch or course. Groundsmanship
is a highly skilled job. Groundsmen maintain pitches for several
sports – bowls, cricket, football, rugby, tennis and so on. Their
duties include tractor- and hand-mowing, marking out and
repairing pitches and keeping them in tip-top condition for
matches. Greenkeepers are specialists employed by golf clubs.
See John Ledgwidge's account on pages 49 and 56.

HEALTH CLUB MANAGER AND ASSISTANT MANAGER

This job can vary considerably in different clubs. Some managers
do some fitness training themselves, while others concentrate on
managing and developing the business. They are responsible for
recruiting and training staff, organising staff rotas, making sure
that the club meets health and safety requirements and
procedures, managing a budget for staff salaries, purchase and
maintenance of equipment, plus advertising and marketing. They
also find out exactly what their customers want by talking to them
or devising questionnaires, then make sure that these activities
are included. They also deal with any requests and complaints.

They are usually on a profit-related salary and have to achieve
certain targets.

CASE STUDY

Sue Hornibrook, Assistant Manager, Bannatyne's Health Club
Bannatyne Fitness Ltd is a health club chain with 32 clubs across
the country and it is still expanding. Sue is assistant manager at
Bannatyne's in Ingleby Barwick near Stockton-on-Tees. The club
is open from 6.30am until 10pm during the week and from 8am
until 9.30pm at weekends. It also has a licensed bar, which keeps
normal pub hours.

'We have a fully equipped gym with cardio-vascular equipment, resistance equipment and free weights, a pool, sauna, steam room, sunbed and spa, an aerobics suite, a spinning room, a hair and beauty salon, which is franchised out, and a café bar. My role is to assist the general manager to make sure that all these facilities operate smoothly. It is a very interesting job because there are different departments – Reception, Customer Relations, Administration, Fitness Membership, Catering, Domestic Services and a crèche. There are 35 full-time members of staff. Each department has its own head. The heads of department work out their own staffing rotas and there is a duty manager on at all times. I work out their rotas.

'I work the same shifts as the staff, so I could be working 6am–3pm, 3pm–11.30pm or 9.00am–6pm. I spend about half my time on paperwork and for the rest of the time I am out and about. I usually do three or four 'walk rounds', checking that all the staff are in the right place and wearing the correct uniforms, and working through my checklist. I check that the gym staff are in, that pool tests are being done, that all is well in the crèche, that we have fresh flowers, and I may help out where needed. Reception gets very busy so I might spend some time there. If the sales staff are busy I might take a prospective new member on a tour. I'll check the temperature of the pool and sauna myself and look at the daily sales records.

'I also talk to members. I love doing this. It's an enjoyable part of the job and one that is very important. The number of clients in the club at any one time varies, but there is a general pattern. When we open at 6.30 we get people who come before work. In the hours of off-peak membership during the day we get young mums and older members. Then in the evenings we get a lot of younger clients. We run classes throughout the day and many more in the evenings. We do body conditioning, aqua classes, latino (jive), t'ai chi, spinning – this is a very popular activity – tap, Pilates, yoga, fit ball, circuit training and karate. Classes are taken by our own fitness staff who offer classes in the activities they are good at, supplemented by freelance staff who work varying hours. We have a good, dynamic team.

'I like to keep busy and to progress in my career, so I am doing a part-time degree in business studies at Teesside University. This takes up Thursday evenings for lectures – and more time for private study. I am learning things that are directly useful in my work here and which should help me in my ambition, which is to own my own club one day.'

LEISURE ASSISTANT

You would be at the front end, keeping the centre going. Be prepared for hard work, some of it boring – cleaning changing rooms, moving and repairing equipment, getting areas of the centre ready for different activities. It's all essential work – and you are highly unlikely to get a job higher up the ladder until you have experience at this level. The job, which involves meeting clients and has variety, can be satisfying in itself. However, promotion prospects are good if you want to work hard and take additional qualifications.

Leisure assistants might sometimes help out at reception, answering the telephone, taking bookings and hiring out equipment like racquets. They might also take turns working in the cafés and bar, serving food and drinks and running children's birthday parties – organising games or swimming and supervising tea.

You can read more about this job in *Careers 2005*, published by Trotman. (See Sources of information at the end of this book.)

CASE STUDY

Adam Dodd, Leisure Assistant, Cocks Moors Woods Centre, Birmingham

Adam's responsibilities include working as a lifeguard, setting up the sports hall, looking after equipment, ensuring the general cleanliness of the centre and looking after the public who use the leisure centre.

He keeps up to date with regular training. Staff receive two hours' training every fortnight, and an update of his National Pool Lifeguard Qualification every two months ensures that Adam always has the most up-to-date knowledge in this field. He has also undertaken training in first aid at work, health and safety, spinal injuries, lifting and handling, complaints handling and customer care.

He has recently been selected for training as a future manager. His next career move would be to gain promotion to senior leisure assistant, then assistant manager and eventually centre manager. He is doing as much personal development and getting as many qualifications as he can in order to achieve this goal.

On a typical day Adam will start by checking all the areas that the public will be using, making sure that the alarms are working and that the changing areas are clean and safe. He will then be on duty, walking around the centre checking that everything is running smoothly. Adam also has poolside duty every day. There are normally four leisure assistants on duty at the pool at any time, and they are not only responsible for the safety of the bathers and spectators, but must also check that each other is all right. If one of them has to perform a rescue, then they will need the support of the rest of the team to manage the situation.

The enjoyable side

One of the aspects that Adam enjoys the most about his job is meeting people and dealing with the public. 'You need to like talking to people or this job would be very difficult as it is very rare to have a day when you don't need to advise someone or maybe deal with a complaint.' There is a good atmosphere where he works and this is one of the reasons he really enjoys his job. He works in a supportive team and says they do activities both in and out of work that help build up trust and cooperation between them. 'When you are dealing with the safety of the public and handling emergency situations, you need to be able to trust your colleagues and know what they are capable of.'

And the downsides

One of the things that Adam doesn't like so much is the rota system. 'Working shifts makes it hard to plan things, but you do get used to it quite quickly.' He works 36.5 hours per week on a three-week shift rotation, which means that he gets every third weekend off.

Adam's advice
'You should get as many qualifications as possible if you want to move up the career ladder. It is also useful to get yourself into a leisure environment as soon as possible – maybe getting a part-time job whilst you are studying. Academic qualifications are really important, but you also need to learn how to deal with the public, and you can learn a lot from other more experienced people.'

LEISURE CENTRE MANAGER

The work is very similar to that described by Sue Hornibrook, who works in a health club, but is likely to be done in a much larger centre where there will be a general manager and several assistant managers, who each take charge of some aspects of running the centre. A large leisure centre might hold children's parties, rent rooms for receptions, conferences and exhibitions and have a number of coffee shops and restaurants, and a beauty salon, in addition to sports courts and fitness suites.

You can find more information about this career in *Careers 2005*, published by Trotman. (See Sources of information at the end of this book.)

LIFEGUARD/POOL/ATTENDANT

Pool attendants patrol the side of the pool (or sit in the chair), looking out for swimmers who seem hesitant or likely to get into difficulties and watching to make sure that no one runs along the side of the pool or jumps into the water in a dangerous way. If anyone is in danger in the water, the pool attendant first throws them a rope or flotation aid and helps them to the edge. If necessary, one attendant dives in to perform a rescue while another asks all other swimmers to leave the pool. They may have to perform resuscitation at the side of the pool. They must hold the National Pool Lifeguard Qualification – although the Royal Life Saving Society's bronze medallion could be accepted as an alternative.

They might be responsible for pool maintenance, which involves checking levels of chemicals and water temperature. In some leisure centres they may also work as general leisure assistants and have a mix of pool and dryside duties.

- The Royal Lifesaving Society has over 60,000 lifeguards on its database and trains over 30,000 pool and beach lifeguards each year.

- Lifeguards are employed by local councils, leisure centres, private clubs, hotels and holiday centres.

- With further training, lifeguards may advance to supervisory and management roles.

You can read more about this career in *Careers 2005,* published by Trotman. (See Sources of information at the end of this book.)

OUTDOOR PURSUITS INSTRUCTOR

Instructors specialise in one or more activities such as mountaineering, rock climbing, orienteering, riding or water sports such as sailing, canoeing and windsurfing, and teach them to small groups of people. They need professional qualifications such as those from the British Canoe Association, the Mountain Leader Training Board or the Royal Yachting Association. Most instructors work in residential centres where clients visit while on holiday.

- There are around 78,000 outdoor pursuits instructors, who can find opportunities throughout the country. However, there is severe competition for posts.

- There are almost as many seasonal and casual jobs as permanent ones in outdoor activities.

- More men than women work in outdoor activities.

You can read more about this career in *Careers 2005,* published by Trotman. (See Sources of information at the end of this book.)

CASE STUDY

Claire Coomer, PE Teacher
Claire has been teaching at John Hanson Secondary (comprehensive) School in Andover, Hampshire, for two terms. Before starting this job she had a varied career.

Claire first did a degree in Sports Science at Brighton University. On leaving, she decided to work for a Master's degree in Sports Psychology and fund herself through working as a tennis coach. (She had qualified as a tennis coach on her degree course.) It didn't work out, though. 'Somehow I seemed to take on more and more hours of coaching and the degree work got left behind! Eventually I became a full-time coach. I did that for two years – then worked in a leisure centre in Guildford where I worked as a tennis coach and a sports development officer.'

Claire then decided to teach. She was offered a job at her old college: and since the college catered for students over the statutory school-leaving age, it was not essential for her to be a qualified teacher. The college gave her time to study for a City and Guilds Further Education Certificate, then a Certificate in Education.

Claire taught 16- to 19-year-old students doing A-level Sports Studies, the college's own Sports Certificate course, GCSE Human Physiology and some modules on the Intermediate GNVQ (General National Vocational Qualification, now replaced by Vocational GCSE) in Leisure and Tourism. 'Seventy per cent of my work was teaching theory. Not being trained or having done teaching practice, I found it difficult to assess how much material I would cover in one lesson. There was a lot of marking to do too. I would work late, get up early and spend the whole of every half-term week trying to get ahead.' It was rewarding, however. 'The students had all chosen to come to college and to do the courses. They were all volunteers and all enthusiastic.' Claire also ran the college ladies' football team (who became county champions) and coached the men's football teams ('this was pretty rare'), indoor hockey and tennis. In her spare time (!) she coached juniors at the local tennis club.

The college decided to offer a two-year full-time BTEC National Diploma in Sports Studies – and Claire, still only in her third year of teaching, was appointed course leader. What did this involve?

'It meant a lot of paperwork and a lot of tracking! The students had to do a number of different modules, some of which I and the other two PE teachers taught and some of which were taught by staff from other departments. I actually had a course team of seven. I was so lucky in the other staff! We all knew each other well – and most of them did sport themselves. We had a couple of formal meetings each term but we had lots of informal ones. I could say to Clare who taught maths for instance that we had just done fitness assessments and produced an enormous amount of data which she could then use in the students' maths course. I could tell the IT lecturer (also a sportsman) that the students had to do a presentation for me – and he would teach them Powerpoint. It all integrated very well.'

Last year Claire left the college for a new job. 'I felt it was time for a change. I had no school experience. I was not a qualified teacher for the statutory age group – and it was important to get QTS (Qualified Teacher Status) if I wanted to work abroad. I have two ambitions – one to do that Master's degree in Sports Psychology (but this time on a full-time course) and the other to work in Australia at some point. I got the job at John Hanson and, because of my previous experience, have been able to qualify part-time through the Graduate Teaching Programme.'

Work in a secondary school is very different from that in a post-16 college. For a start the atmosphere is very different. 'From the moment the pupils arrive at 8.15 until they leave at 3.15 it is non-stop. There is more structure to the day – and no free time at all.' Claire takes lessons in hockey, volleyball, badminton, orienteering, tennis, cricket, athletics, netball, rounders and football, in addition to teaching a junior sports leader award course, GCSE PE and GCSE science. Next year she will be part of a team of staff teaching Personal and Social Education. 'I shall be covering health education – topics like drugs, drink, contraception and so on. I'm looking forward to it.'

PERSONAL TRAINER

In this role you would do the same sort of activities as a fitness instructor but, instead of taking classes, you'd work with one person at a time.

CASE STUDY

Christianne Wolff, Personal Trainer

Christianne's clients include film stars, pop stars, TV presenters, models and company directors. Among them are Pierce Brosnan,

Dougray Scott (Mission Impossible 2), Martha Lane-Fox, founder of lastminute.com – and many others whose names she can't reveal. (In this job discretion and maintaining client confidentiality are essential.).

She has an impressive list of qualifications – in aerobics, circuit training, body conditioning, indoor rock climbing, Khai-Bo, marathon/triathlon, Pilates, weight lifting/training, yoga, spinning, pre- and post-natal exercise, step and exercise to music.

How did she begin?
'I am very fortunate in that I have been able to convert a barn owned by my parents and therefore have my own gym! I bought the equipment quite cheaply through e-bay. There are some good bargains if you know what you are looking for and I now have a rower, treadmill, crosstrainer, parachute runner, barbells, steps and a bench.' But, she points out, it is not necessary to own all this equipment. Some personal trainers pay a fee to use a commercial gym when working with clients; others work in their clients' homes. When Christianne does home visits she carries only skipping ropes and Swiss balls in her car. Some of her clients have bought their own equipment. 'If they can afford to pay me they can also afford an exercise bike or other pieces of equipment.'

How does she decide on a programme for each client?
'At our first meeting I work through a questionnaire with them. I establish their past exercise history, get a medical history and ask what they hope to achieve and in what space of time. I do a fitness test, take blood pressure, test fat/muscle ratio, and conduct a strength test. Then we knuckle down to setting goals. Do they want to improve general fitness? Lose weight? Train for a particular event? Are they being realistic? Some of my clients are high achievers and used to getting fast results! I have to explain that in this situation they'll have to compromise. I then draw up an exercise plan that includes work they will do with me and work to do on their own. I think this is important. Clients shouldn't get too dependent on me and need me there all the time.'

Some of her clients come through the website of the National Register of Personal Trainers but the majority now come through word of mouth. She also teaches four classes each week – and gets more individual clients or recommendations there.

Christianne has developed her career in several directions. She now spends most of her time working with individual clients, has her four weekly classes – and spends about ten per cent of her time writing on fitness topics. She is also about to launch, through her own website, a service for people who want to work with a personal trainer in their own homes, using a personally tailored programme.

'I was lucky when I qualified to land a part-time job at Pineapple Dance Studios in Covent Garden. It has a high profile and a lot of celebrities go there; consequently it is where media scouts tend to go if they are looking for a fitness expert. As a result a production company has asked me to present a fitness video and I have done some TV work.' She has also moved into fitness journalism – but through a more down-to-earth method. 'I was working in a health club one day when a reporter from the local paper came in looking for someone to write some articles for no payment. I had never written before, but I agreed to try. I had some articles published – then sent the cuttings to other magazines. This has brought me work from *M-Celebs*, the *Evening Standard Magazine*, *Health and Fitness* and *Men's Fitness* magazines.

You can find out more about Christianne's work at www.designerworkout.com.

This is life at the top end. Many personal trainers are able to charge £60 per hour and more. Others earn around £30 an hour and do not enjoy the benefit of having their own gym.

THE DOWNSIDES
You would have to pay for your own training in order to get an approved qualification. (But you could do so part-time while working in another job.) You would need to allow for expenses like hire of space in a gym *or* budget for your own car so that you could work in clients' homes. Other expenses would include professional insurance and repairs to or replacement of equipment.

You would need to be able to handle money and to budget. Most personal trainers also do some coaching or take classes – for which they are paid regularly. You would also work very unsocial hours.

PROFESSIONAL SPORTSPERSON

Only a few very talented people make their living in team sports – mainly in football, cricket, basketball, rugby, ice hockey and hockey. Other sports that are played professionally include boxing, cycling, golf, motor racing, horse racing, snooker, show jumping, rugby and speedway riding. In some sports, people often turn professional in their teens, although in cricket some players wait until they are in their 20s to do so. (It is possible to have a full-time career in test and county cricket.) There are approximately 630 first-class cricketers under contract to 18 county clubs. The majority are aged between 18 and 35.

A playing career is short and is usually over by the age of 40. All professional players start playing their sport when they are young and work through the ranks of school teams, club and county teams, then playing at national level. In some sports – football is one – talent scouts and coaches visit sports events looking for young players with high potential. The age at which young people can start varies in different sports. Boys can join football's Associated Schoolboy Scheme from 14, whereas players often start in cricket and golf in their early 20s. Tennis players are classed as adults at 16. Professional sportspeople earn appearance fees and prize money. Famous players increase their income by advertising products.

Currently, there are more opportunities for men in professional sport than there are for women. This could change as more women play traditionally masculine sports such as football, and we could see more professional opportunities for women.

Golf is increasing in popularity in the UK, particularly among young people. More golf courses are being opened, so there is a growing demand for golf professionals. Golf professional is a confusing term, since there are actually two types of professional player. Tournament players play on the circuits and earn an income from prize money and sponsorship. To become tournament players, golfers must obtain a qualifying card. Competition is severe. Professional golfers must be members of the Professional Golfers' Association (PGA). They have to pass exams and demonstrate excellent playing ability to be accepted.

Matt Stevens (see page 66) refers to his coach as a club professional. Club professionals are attached to a golf club. They help with administration, work in the golf shop, repair equipment, and may coach club members. There are around 2,200 club professionals in the United Kingdom, around 30 of whom are women.

You can read more about careers in professional sport in *Careers 2005*, published by Trotman. (See Sources of information at the end of this book.)

FASCINATING FACTS

- Wayne Rooney is the youngest footballer to gain a full cap, aged 17 (for England against Turkey in 2003.) His predecessor was Michael Owen, who was crowned the youngest player to receive a full cap, at age 18 (for England against Chile in 1998).

- Paula Radcliffe is fluent in French and Italian and translates sports journals into English to keep her language skills up.

- Both Venus and Serena Williams studied fashion design at the Art Institute of Florida.

- Ellen Macarthur has set up a trust to support and encourage young people who have cancer or leukaemia by taking them on sailing trips.

- Tiger Woods is the first player to win the Jack Nicklaus award for four consecutive years.

SPORTS DEVELOPMENT WORK

People who used to play a sport but haven't done so for years may be looking for a way to get back into the game. Many sports clubs need help in starting up, recruiting new members, getting hold of grants and training their coaches. Many people would like to become coaches. Sports development officers make sure that as many people as possible are provided with the information and support that they need – whatever their sport.

CASE STUDY

Kevin Harris, Sports Development Officer (SDO), Southampton City Council

What does his job involve?

'SDOs' work varies according to their level of seniority and also according to how the work is organised in the authority they work for. There are three of us here: the Senior SDO who does more administrative and high-level work; another SDO who does general development work and also specialises in developing swimming; and myself. My remit is to develop coaching, and provide information and advice to sports practitioners.

'So I have a very diverse role that includes anything from answering a simple phone enquiry about the whereabouts of tennis clubs to helping community groups apply for funds to running coaching education programmes. I work with teachers, sports coaches, sports clubs, individuals and groups across the city. I spend a major part of my time on advice concerned with fundraising. If a group of people wants to start a club for instance I advise them which organisation to approach and help them with the application. The coaching education programme is very important. Coaches are volunteers, giving up their evenings and weekends. Without them many sporting activities would not happen. So it is essential to provide them support. I run monthly sessions for them in conjunction with a local higher education institution. I am also organising a special series of events for them this month as a Sports Coaches' Roadshow.

'I enjoy my job and count myself lucky to have found it. It does involve unsocial hours – I have to go to weekend coaching events and evening meetings. For example, I am going to one tonight with a community group that has got funding, with our help, to launch a football coaching programme for children in a deprived area. The hope is to give them something positive to do instead of hanging round the streets and potentially getting into trouble. But I can always have time off when other people are working.'

'When I started my degree course I was unsure about a future career. In the second year I had the option of specialising in sports development or sport and recreation management. I chose sports development because I was interested in the sociological and cultural development aspects of sport. Eventually I decided that this was what I wanted to do.'

Kevin's Sports Coaches' Roadshow programme
Monday, 6–8pm
Periodisation Workshop
Tuesday 5.30–9.30pm
Emergency Aid Certificate
Thursday 6.30–8.30pm
Speed, Agility and Quickness (SAQ) taster session
Monday 6.30–9.30pm
Sports Coach UK Workshop – Injury prevention and management
Wednesday, 6.30–9.30 pm
Sport England Running Sport Workshop – Volunteer management

Kevin's department has a website (www.southampton.gov.uk/ Leisure/Sports), from which you can learn more about his and his colleagues' work. It also has a Student Zone, which gives advice to people who would like to become sports development officers. Although it refers to opportunities in Southampton it contains useful information on getting into this career – and finding opportunities for voluntary work. You might find that your own local council has a similar website.

SWIMMING TEACHER
Swimming teachers give lessons to learners and to swimmers who are working for medals and lifesaving awards. They might also coach swimmers for competitions. Some of their lessons are

given to groups; others to individuals. They may go in the water with their pupils or may instruct from the side of the pool. Some swimming teachers are employed by leisure centres and combine the work with that of a pool attendant, lifeguard or leisure centre assistant. Others are self-employed.

OPPORTUNITIES TO WORK OVERSEAS

Once you have some qualifications under your belt you might want to spread your wings and see a bit of the world. Doing this could be a temporary thing – or you could even work abroad permanently. How?

Look at temporary and seasonal jobs for instructors in:

● hotels and campsites

● residential summer camps for children

● outdoor pursuits centres

● sailing schools

● water sports schools.

Fitness and exercise instructors can find work in centres in international hotel chains, in private clubs or on passenger cruise ships. Teachers can work in many countries – in British or international schools. There are a lot of sailing and water sports centres in other countries – and British qualifications are respected.

MEDIA JOBS RELATED TO SPORT

JOURNALIST
Very few journalists earn a living by writing about sport alone. Only national newspapers employ specialists. The majority of journalists are employed on local papers where they cover sport in addition to general news stories and other special-interest topics. There are also opportunities to write for magazines – usually as a freelance.

There are different routes into careers as sports journalists. Some people train first as journalists, then become specialists in sport. Others develop expertise in a sport or play professionally, then try their hand at writing and get into journalism that way.

● TV sports reporter Rob Bonnet started his career in local radio. From there he moved to presenting programmes for national radio, then to television. He spent eight years as a sports reporter for BBC News and now presents sports news on BBC Breakfast, BBC1 at weekends and BBC World.

● Personal trainer Christianne Wolff accepted a request to write some articles on fitness for a newspaper – for no fee. She moved on to being able to charge for her work.

● Former professional cricketer David Gower writes on cricket for national newspapers.

SPORTS PHOTOGRAPHER

As with journalism, it is usual to qualify first as a photographer, then specialise. Photographers may be employed by one newspaper, by an agency that submits pictures to a number of papers, or may be freelance. It is possible to train in general photography, or to do a specialist training course in press photography that is recognised by the National Council for the Training of Journalists.

MEDICAL WORK RELATED TO SPORT AND FITNESS

NUTRITIONIST

Some people take short qualifications in nutrition and diet for a healthy lifestyle and use them in their work as coaches or trainers. There is also a much longer training course – a degree – which leads to work as a nutritionist or dietician with people who have all kinds of illnesses and dietary problems.

OSTEOPATH

Osteopaths treat injuries by manipulating bones and joints. It is not possible to train purely as a sports osteopath. A full-time osteopathy course must be taken first.

The entry qualifications, training and work of an osteopath are described fully in *Getting Into Healthcare Professions*, published by Trotman.

SPORT AND EXERCISE SCIENTIST OR PHYSIOLOGIST

Performers and coaches sometimes employ sport and exercise scientists who use their specialist training to improve aspects of training and reduce the risk of injury. They might also suggest adjustments to training programmes or changes of equipment. They often work as freelance consultants.

You can read more about this career in *Careers 2005*, published by Trotman. (See Sources of information at the end of this book.)

SPORTS PHYSIOTHERAPIST

Sports physiotherapists treat a wide range of sport-related injuries and strains. They use a range of treatments, including manipulation, massage, heat treatment, therapeutic exercise, electrotherapy, ultrasound, acupuncture and hydrotherapy.

Some sports physiotherapists work only with professional sportspeople. (There are some full-time opportunities in professional sport – but many physiotherapists who work with sports teams are volunteers.) Others work with amateur sportspeople and people who take part in sport as a leisure activity. Many of those who hold sports injuries clinics – perhaps in leisure and recreation centres – are either self-employed or are already employed in hospitals. The increasing interest in sport is leading to more opportunities for sports physiotherapists. It is not possible to train solely for sports physiotherapy. You would have to qualify first in general physiotherapy – which is a much broader profession. This means taking a physiotherapy degree approved by the Health Professions Council. During your training you would treat all kinds of patients in clinics and on wards. You would have to be prepared, for example, to help some cough up fluid from their lungs after operations and to coax reluctant ones out of bed to exercise after hip or similar operations.

CASE STUDY

Gill Driver, Physiotherapist, Winchester, Hampshire
Gill works for three days a week in a clinic at the city's leisure centre and spends one day teaching physiotherapy students at Southampton University. She also has two children. Gill did her degree course at Queen Elizabeth Hospital, Birmingham, then moved to Southampton General Hospital, where she had two posts on grades known as Junior and Senior II. In these grades newly qualified physiotherapists do what is known as rotations – periods spent in gaining experience in different specialities. For her first rotations, each lasting four months, Gill chose to do orthopaedics, neurosurgery, intensive care, cardiothoracic, paediatrics and work with the elderly. She followed these by eight-month rotations in the gym (where she treated lower limbs), hydrotherapy, and the treatment room – treating spines, backs, necks and shoulders. Next came a move to Bournemouth as a Senior I to gain experience in GP practices. She could have gone on to specialise in any of those areas, and made a career in the NHS, but she had decided by this point that she wanted to work in private practice and to specialise in sports injuries work.

'While I was in Bournemouth I did some sports injury and other private work in the evenings. On moving to Winchester I worked for 18 hours a week in the NHS – and at the same time worked part-time for a friend who had a private practice. I also began to work here. It was hard work! You cannot just walk into private practice. You have to build up the work gradually and keep your main job until you are confident that you can go it alone. When I started, if patients wanted appointments on a Saturday afternoon, they got them. I couldn't turn any away. I was working from 7am until 9pm on many days.

'Now, I work with four other physiotherapists, all of whom do a certain number of sessions here and have other jobs too. We are completely independent and are not employed by the leisure centre. We rent the rooms (treatment room and office) and have bought all the equipment ourselves. Only one of us is here at a time but we do communicate by phone and meet occasionally. We used to do all our own administration but have just taken someone on to do that so that we can concentrate on patient care. Between us we keep the clinic open from 9am to 5pm and from 6pm to 8pm.

'Anyone who wants private physiotherapy can consult us; they do not have to be suffering from sports injuries. I would say that about half my patients have sports injuries and the remainder come with all kinds of problems. I regularly use the whole range of treatments and give re-education and exercise advice.

'Patients come by GP referral, word of mouth, and many come simply because we are in the sports centre. The patients I see who do have sports injuries come with a number of different problems, including strains or damage to tendons, muscles, ligaments and cartilage. They might have injured themselves on a sports court or pitch or they may come because they are suffering from an injury that affects their ability to do sport. They might notice pain from a previous injury or condition that makes an exercise class painful, for instance. I see a lot of people with back and neck problems and posture-related pain.

'I love my job and feel that I have the best of both worlds. I can work just as hard as I choose to. I can fit my work around collecting the children from school. Very important to me is the fact that I am still using all my skills and am still "hands on". As you move up the ladder in general physiotherapy you have more management and administrative work to do and less patient contact. I still have that. There are other satisfactions. I can spend as long as I need to with each patient. In a NHS hospital they would only be able to have a certain number of sessions. And we do not have waiting lists. We can usually offer appointments on the same day that someone makes a request.

'There are drawbacks, of course. I have no paid holidays or sick leave. If I were ill I would have no cover, whereas in a hospital someone else would pick up some of the cases. I can't be ill. Patients expect me to be here! I have to pay for my own continuing professional development. My professional association, the Organisation for Chartered Physiotherapists in Private Practice, requires members to spend 25 hours a year in training and updating skills. If I worked in a hospital this would be paid for. A possible downside could be professional isolation because I am not working with colleagues every day. But I do have my day a week at the university and can exchange ideas and discuss cases with colleagues there.'

What skills does Gill need in her job?
'Other than the technical skills, communication is the most important. We have to be able to establish relationships with patients and their relatives. We work with patients of all ages and we also have to build working relationships with doctors and consultants.'

SPORTS PSYCHOLOGIST
Sports psychologists help amateur and professional players to improve their performance through the use of psychological techniques. Teachers, coaches and personal trainers all use psychology in their work. Opportunities to work solely as a sports psychologist are limited – and although there are some people who earn a living from this work alone, many others are also teachers, lecturers or researchers, or work in a combination of all these jobs. A major part of the work is concerned with trying to improve a team's or an individual performer's motivation.

CASE STUDY

Kieran Kingston, Sports Psychologist
'The value of psychology in sport is increasingly recognised – but even so there are limited opportunities for sports psychologists to practise as full-time consultants. I have colleagues who work full-time but most, like myself, do a combination of this and other work in sports psychology, such as teaching or research. I do all three. I am a senior lecturer in sports psychology at the University of Wales Institute, Cardiff (UWIC), am involved in a number of ongoing research projects and, when time permits, work with groups and individuals as a sports psychologist. My main focus in this work is with elite golfers – both professional and amateur – and with professional snooker players. My clients come from different sources – referrals from colleagues, from golf clubs (I play locally), from the BASES (British Association for Sport and

Exercise Science) register, which anyone who is looking for a sports psychologist can consult, and most of all through word of mouth.

'In my opinion, the principal role of sports psychologists is to provide players with tools to help them perform better. It can involve facilitating the development of strategies to help them become more effective when training or competing or involve mental preparation and development of competition plans. Much of the work is what we call 'Band Aid' – that is, a player will come with a specific problem. For example, a professional athlete might seek out my support to deal with competition nerves that are undermining his/her performance. Initially, I am seeking to gather information. What are the triggers to the occurrence of the nervous reaction? How long have they been occurring? How does this state differ from when he/she performs well? What (if anything) is done differently before situations when the nerves cause performance to drop, as opposed to when they do not get in the way? I am trying to start to understand the nature of the condition and the underlying causes; the athlete will also (I hope) come to develop a greater self-awareness, which in itself can serve as the start of the therapeutic process. Once we are both comfortable that we are starting to understand and even rationalise the causes, I will work on strategies to alleviate the "issue".

'An important part of a sports psychologist's work is to establish a relationship with a client and to look holistically at the problem that presents. Does the player have problems outside sport and need support in other areas for instance? You must be able to make them feel comfortable with you and ready to open up. It may also be the case that the issues are beyond your area of expertise, in which case you might refer the athlete to another professional such as a clinical psychologist. Recognising and accepting your own limitations is an important aspect of the consultancy role.

'Work with groups is different. I do seminars and workshops for small groups of sports bursary students at Cardiff University. Here, I take on more of an educational role and do not concentrate on any specific problems. Again, my role is to help these athletes acquire skills to assist their performance. I am also contracted to the PGA for whom I also do workshops and lectures – for elite coaches and registered professional players. I have just returned from giving a series of workshops in Edinburgh.'

CHAPTER 3

How do I get into sport and fitness?

It all depends on what stage you are at right now. There is more than one way of getting into most jobs. Those in sport and fitness are no exception. You can nearly always find your way into a career area whether you leave school at 16 or 18, or go on to higher education. However, a career in professional sport does require you to have made an early start – playing for amateur teams, competing in events, etc.

SOME PEOPLE WORKING IN SPORT AND FITNESS AND HOW THEY STARTED

'I didn't really enjoy school all that much and left after the first year of A-levels. I found a Modern Apprenticeship placement myself at Ipswich Town Football Club and worked on a programme called Community Challenge. I did some coaching and helped to teach basic life skills – and really enjoyed both.'

Andy Crump, Modern Apprentice

Adam Dodd, Leisure Assistant, Cocks Moors Woods Centre, Birmingham

Adam obtained an Advanced GNVQ (now Vocational A-levels) in Leisure and Tourism at sixth-form college. He originally wanted a career as a hotel manager, and worked part-time at the Belfry Hotel in Sutton Coldfield to gain experience during his studies. Unfortunately they didn't have a full-time position for him when he left college, but Adam had by then started getting interested in the leisure side of things and had completed his lifesaving qualification. He applied for the position of leisure assistant and was successful. He has now been working as a leisure assistant for four years.

Although the interview for the position itself was fairly informal, Adam had to demonstrate his knowledge and skills in several areas, including swimming two lengths in under a minute, and demonstrating his first aid knowledge. It was also essential that he had his NPLQ (National Pool Lifeguard Qualification), as lifeguard work forms a large part of his responsibilities.

John Ledgwidge, Modern Apprentice

John left school in 2002 with 10 GCSE grades A and B but instead of entering the sixth form or attending college full-time, he opted to live out his lifelong dream. He had set his heart on becoming a groundskeeper at the age of 13 – and successfully gained an apprenticeship at Coventry City FC by writing directly to the club. Although he was only 16, he had already been working as a volunteer at City for two years, so the head groundskeeper decided to give him the opportunity to train as a Foundation Modern Apprentice.

CASE STUDY

Kevin Harris, Sports Development Officer

Kevin has a degree in sports studies from University College, Chichester. During the course he was able to take a sports development pathway. Like many other people in this book he discovered that the way into the job he wanted involved first gaining experience through voluntary work. It also involved hard graft! At one stage he was working 39 hours a week in a full-time job and as a volunteer.

'I soon found that you don't leave university and just walk into a job! It hit me that I needed a lot more experience and that voluntary work was the way to get it. I took a full-time clerical job, selling membership of fitness clubs and contacted this department to see if I could come in and help out on a voluntary basis. The hours in my full-time job were flexible, so I was able to juggle them over a 39-hour week and come in here to do some of the administrative work and help out with projects.

'I had gained football coaching qualifications on my degree course, so I also applied for some paid coaching jobs. I got a position with Southampton City Football Club, coaching on their Football in the Community Programme. I worked all over the city, bringing quality coaching to children in after-school clubs in primary schools and in a sports centre on Saturdays. I also coached my girlfriend's brother's football team (13-year-olds) on a voluntary basis. Looking back, I don't know how I fitted it all in! But I cannot stress enough the importance of doing work like this if you want to get into my job.'

Kevin increased his activities during the summer holidays, working weekends with the Hampshire and Isle of Wight Partnership Active Sports Programme, as a development officer for women's and girls' football – 'I had never coached girls before, so it was a new experience' – and on a rugby community project, both of which gave him real sports development experience. He worked for the same partnership at the Hampshire Youth Games. 'This event takes place every year and allows young people to take part in a variety of sports – girls' football, rugby, basketball and so on. There were also the Parallel Games for young people with disabilities. I ran a disabled players' football tournament.'

All this work gave Kevin experience – but equally valuable was the opportunity to network. He got to know sports development officers and his work became known. So when a vacancy for a sports development officer came up with the city council he applied for a job which he already knew and understood. Ironically, at this point Kevin had applied for and been accepted to do a Master's degree in Sport on Wednesday afternoons. He managed to convince the interviewers that it would be good for the department if he gained this qualification - and was allowed to do so, provided that he worked his full week of 37.5 hours. So once again Kevin is doing more than one job.

SUE HORNIBROOK, ASSISTANT MANAGER, BANNATYNE'S HEALTH CLUB
Sue has always been interested in sport and is a qualified gymnastics coach. When she left school, however, she became a receptionist with a computer company.

'Office work was not enough for me. I enjoyed the work but wanted to do the same job in an environment that interested me more. When Bannatyne's opened I came here as a receptionist. I was promoted to reception manager at the club in Durham – then, when an opening became available, came back here to manage Reception. The manager saw that I was keen to progress and offered to let me do the assistant manager training course. Then, while I was still doing it, the job became vacant. I applied and was successful.'

Gill Driver, Physiotherapist
Gill started out by training as a physiotherapist and working in the NHS. She then set up her own private practice by working evenings and weekends in sports injury work. When she had enough private work she left the NHS.

CASE STUDY

Kieran Kingston, Sports Psychologist

'My first step was to do a degree in physical education at University of Wales, Bangor, with the aim of becoming a PE teacher. I became interested in sports psychology during my second year when we did some modules in the subject, and went on to do my third-year project on "Focus of attention while executing a sport skill". I then decided that I wanted a career consisting of teaching, research and work with athletes. My first step was to enrol on a research-based part-time Master's in Sports Psychology – funded through part-time teaching.

'As a result of a presentation I made I was invited to the University of North Carolina as a visiting scholar. At the time, I was undecided on whether I wanted to pursue a doctorate (to be honest, it always seemed like something that intellectuals got involved with, and I never, and still don't, view myself in that manner). However, by the time I returned from the US I had decided that I wanted to continue and develop my research ideas, and attempt to complete a PhD. While doing all my academic work I did the BASES qualifications in sports psychology, which involved getting a minimum of three years' supervised experience working with different athletes. After combining my doctoral studies with a full-time teaching job, I moved to a university teaching position at Liverpool for one year, and then came to Cardiff in 2000.'

AND SOME CELEBS

Paula Radcliffe started running at the age of seven when she ran for one mile with her father, a marathon runner. Aged nine, she joined Bedford Athletics Club. In her first national race as a schoolgirl, she came in 299th! But she believed that if she persisted she could do it in the end. She trained hard, entered events – and never gave up. She put up with comments about being the person who always finished just outside the medals – and went on to win the London Marathon at her first attempt. In the same year she became the European 10,000 metres and the Commonwealth 5,000 metres champion. She still has the coach she met at the Bedford Club.

Venus and Serena Williams started winning tennis tournaments when they were ten years old. Everyone knows that they trained on public courts, coached by their father. They had professional coaching at one point, but then returned to their father who continued to coach them and to manage their careers. He insisted that they both finished high school rather than concentrate on their junior tennis circuit – and both went on to art school.

Ellen Macarthur was inspired by sailing trips she made with her aunt when she was aged eight. She saved up for three years to buy her first boat, which was an eight-foot dinghy. She sailed around Britain on her own aged 18. Sailors need equipment (a boat, obviously!) and sponsorship. Ellen lived in a Portakabin for three years while saving to buy a Classe Mini yacht and raising sponsorship to compete in a transatlantic race.

Jonny Wilkinson was inspired by his father, a rugby player, who took him to Farnham Minis when he was five. He was hooked immediately. He never gave any other career a serious thought. He knew he wanted to be a rugby professional – and turned down a university place in order to sign a two-year contract with Newcastle. Today, he is apparently always the first one on to the training field and the last one off!

Do these stars demonstrate determination, or what?

WHAT ARE YOU GOING TO DO?

Here are a few different entry routes.

MODERN APPRENTICESHIPS
These are available in: Sports and Recreation; and the Horse Industry.

You can find out which might be available in your area from your Connexions personal adviser or careers adviser.

In England and Wales, Foundation Modern Apprenticeships are for anyone aged 16–24 who has left full-time education and has not yet found work, or who is already in employment. There is no set time limit for completing an apprenticeship but all programmes last at least 12 months. Most people enter them at 16 or 17 but you can also take further qualifications first. There is a second programme – the Advanced Modern Apprenticeship in England or Modern Apprenticeship in Wales – that lasts at least 24 months.

Most apprentices are counted as employees and are paid a wage – the going rate for the job. Others are linked to a training provider and are paid a minimum allowance (currently £40 a week). Most employers now offer more than the minimum.

Modern Apprentices follow a training programme consisting of work experience and training for the job. They achieve National Vocational Qualification (NVQ) at level 2, Key Skills and a technical certificate. When they complete the programme, they might decide to progress to an Advanced Modern Apprenticeship/Modern Apprenticeship.

This higher-level apprenticeship trains people up to NVQ Level 3 and is for people who are aiming to work at supervisory or management level. It is intended for 16- and 17-year-old school and college leavers with the ability to gain high-level skills and qualifications. Some people, however, start programmes at 18 after having taken A-levels.

In Scotland, programmes are known as 'Modern Apprenticeships through Skillseekers' You can find more information on Modern Apprenticeships on the SPRITO website, www.skillsactive.com. There are also some questions designed to help you decide whether an apprenticeship is right for you.

ANDY CRUMP, FORMER MODERN APPRENTICE, IPSWICH TOWN FC

'It's been a big success for me, as I've now got a full-time job here and have almost completed my NVQ at level 2 in Sport and Recreation. The Modern Apprenticeship really worked for me as I could do a job I really enjoyed at the same time as gaining qualifications – and now I have just been appointed a full-time football development officer at the club.

'My job involves helping to run our Community Youth Football League and coaching young people taking part in our holiday coaching and weekly coaching programmes. I love my job.'

CASE STUDY

Claire Bryant, Modern Apprentice

Claire has always had an interest in sports and recreation. She left school with nine GCSE passes and two A-levels (Physical Education and Business Studies) and enrolled on an Advanced Modern Apprenticeship (AMA) programme in Sport and Recreation at the Guildford Leisure Complex, which has over 3 million visitors and has a range of facilities including athletics track, ice rink, leisure pool, competition swimming pool, ten-pin bowling and health and fitness centre.

Claire currently holds the position of Health Suite Supervisor. She has already completed four NVQ units at Levels 3 and 4, Key Skills, and job-related qualifications including Sports Leader Award, Premier Fitness Instructor, Nutrition and Exercise Certificate (NHS) and First Aid at Work.

She has had to do assignments as part of her NVQ work, and three of these – "Supporting the Efficient Use of Resources", "Creating Effective Working Relations" and "Maintaining Sport and Recreation Equipment and Facilities" – have been acknowledged by her manager as contributing to the success of the business. In fact, Claire is regarded by members of senior management as such a strong member of staff that she has recently been seconded to the personnel section of the organisation to carry out project work.

Her ambition after completing her AMA is to set up a personal training business and then to train as a PE teacher. She hopes to start a PE degree in 2005.

JOHN LEDGWIDGE, MODERN APPRENTICE (PITCH), COVENTRY CITY FC

'I chose this route because a Modern Apprenticeship offers practical work experience, training, and a wage. Being a lifelong Sky Blues fan I always wanted to walk on the pitch and play for the team, but after I broke my arm when playing in goal when I was 13, I decided the best option was to try and become a groundskeeper, and that way I could walk on the pitch every day.

'Over the past year I have spent one day a week attending Warwickshire College, at Moreton Morell, working towards an NVQ in Horticulture. I was able to learn every aspect of groundskeeping, maintaining the pitch to Premier League standards. I have now completed my Foundation Modern Apprenticeship, and to celebrate the start of the new football season I will soon be working towards the Advanced Modern Apprenticeship in Amenity Horticulture.'

John is hoping to manage the grounds at the new Sky Blues Academy, looking after seven pitches – four made from grass, two indoor pitches and one artificial surface.

WHAT ARE NVQS?

National Vocational Qualifications are awarded in England and Wales; in Scotland they are called Scottish Vocational Qualifications. They are work-related qualifications that demonstrate what a person is capable of doing. They are available at five levels, ranging from Level 1, designed for new entrants to a career, right up to Level 5, which equates to postgraduate level. You gain S/NVQs not by taking exams but by being assessed at work on how well you perform set tasks. You record your achievements in a portfolio of evidence and get a manager or supervisor to sign each one.

Examples of S/NVQs on offer in sport include:

● Coaching, Teaching and Instructing in Swimming

● Facility Operations

- Sports and Recreation

- Sport and Recreation Supervision and Development.

In fitness you could think about:

- Coaching, Teaching and Instructing Adults in Exercise and Fitness

- Coaching, Teaching and Instructing in Exercise to Music

- Coaching, Teaching and Instructing in Aqua

- Coaching, Teaching and Instructing in Step

- Coaching, Teaching and Instructing in Circuit Training

- Coaching, Teaching and Instructing in Gym.

OTHER INDUSTRY-RELATED QUALIFICATIONS

In the fitness industry it is really, really important to take qualifications that employers (and insurance companies) recognise. Also, the punters want to know that they are being taught or trained by people who know what they are doing! You'll probably have to pay to do these – unless an employer will help out. So you need to know that you are getting value for money. There are some dodgy outfits willing to take your cash and offer impressive-sounding certificates. Always check with the Register of Exercise Professionals that training courses are recognised.

Highly respected are:

YMCA FITNESS INDUSTRY TRAINING
This offers modular courses leading to:

- Personal Trainer Award

- Professional Gym Instructor Award

- Professional Studio Instructor Award.

And short courses (additional modules) in:

- Antenatal and Postnatal Exercise

- Assessor Training

- Cardio Pulmonary resuscitation

- Exercise to Music for the Older Person

- Health and Safety

- People and Programme Management

- Sports Injuries

- Stress Management

- Teaching Exercise and Fitness for Disabled People.

You can complete the awards by attending intensive daytime courses, evening classes, weekend courses – or by doing one module at a time.

ROYAL SOCIETY OF ARTS (RSA)
The RSA offers awards in:

- Aqua

- Circuits

- Exercise to Music

- Gym

- Step.

INSTITUTE OF LEISURE AND AMENITY MANAGEMENT (ILAM)
The institute offers qualifications and membership to people in the leisure industry in general. In sport and recreation you could choose ILAM's:

- First Award

- Certificate in Leisure Operations

- Certificate in Leisure Management

- Diploma in Leisure Management

- Advanced Diploma in Leisure Management.

FULL-TIME COURSES

If you stay on into your school's sixth form or transfer to a sixth-form college or college of further education you could take an A-level or National Diploma in Sport.

VOCATIONAL A-LEVEL IN SPORT

This covers the theory and practice of sport and is divided into units. Six units give you one A-level pass; 12 units give you a double A-level. If you were sure that you wanted a career in sport and fitness you could do the double award.

BTEC NATIONAL DIPLOMA IN SPORT

This covers topics such as:

- Practical Sports Performance

- Psychology for Sports Performance

- Sport in Society

- Sports Injuries

- Training and Fitness.

You can use either of the above as a stepping stone to a higher education course.

HIGHER NATIONAL DIPLOMA (HND) COURSES

HNDs are two-year courses (full-time) or three years (sandwich) which have an entry requirement of one A-level/two Highers or

S/NVQ Level 3. You can also offer approved equivalent qualifications and experience at the discretion of universities and colleges. The A-level need not be the vocational one. Almost any subject is accepted.

Colleges and universities offering HND courses are free to design their own programmes, so content can vary considerably. They do, however, receive guidelines from either Edexcel (formerly the Business and Technology Education Council) or SQA, the Scottish Qualifications Authority. These are two validating bodies that monitor the quality of courses and award the diploma.

Content of a typical Higher National Diploma course in Leisure Management:

● Business Law

● Business Strategy

● Business Systems in Leisure

● Customer Care and Service Quality

● Leisure Organisations and Issues

● Management of People

● Managing Finance

● Marketing and Sales

● Operations Management of Sport and Leisure

● Sports and Leisure Marketing

● Options from: Events Management Pathway; Outdoor Recreation; Sports and Leisure Management.

FOUNDATION DEGREES
These have been available since autumn 2001 and are increasing in number. They are heavily backed by the government, which

encourages institutions to provide them. They are not unlike HNDs in content – and the Department for Education and Skills expects all HND programmes to become foundation degrees in due course. Two major differences at the moment are that foundation degree programmes are drawn up by the universities and colleges that run them and not by BTEC, and they must contain work experience.

If you did a foundation degree you would have the option of entering employment and continuing training there, or of converting the qualification into an honours degree through further study, usually by transfer into the second or third year of a related degree course.

DEGREE COURSES

Most degree courses last three years, with a few taking a year longer and including a year's work experience placement. Entry requirements are either two A-levels/three Highers, or NVQ/SVQ Level 3. Other approved equivalent qualifications and experience are sometimes accepted. Entry grades vary in different institutions – not always because some courses are better than others but because popular universities and college can ask for higher grades!

Content of a typical first degree course in Sports Science:

- Applied Coaching Science
- Basic and Applied Sports Science

- Biomedical Implications of Exercise
- Functional Anatomy

- Fundamentals of Human Nutrition
- Human Physiology

- Measurement and Evaluation of Human Performance
- Metabolic Nutrition

- Metabolism and Endocrinology
- Muscle Function

- Paediatric and Geriatric Exercise Science
- Physical Performance Assessment

- Sensory and Motor
  Physiology

- Sports Psychology.

- Sociological Issues in Sport

A degree course in Physical Education with Qualified Teacher Status comprises:

- Child Development and Learning

- Information and Communication Technology

- Personal and Social Education

- Physical Activities

- Physical Education

- School and Community Partnerships

- School Experience

- The Teacher as a Professional

- Options from: Coaching; Dance; Games; Gymnastics; Health-Focused Studies; Leisure Studies; Special Needs.

SOME DEGREE AND/OR DIPLOMA PROGRAMMES

- Applied Sports Science

- Exercise Physiology

- Fitness and Health

- Golf Course Management

- Health Therapies and Sports Fitness

- Coach Education and Sports Development

- Exercise Science

- Fitness Science

- Health Studies and Sports Management

- Leisure Management

- Leisure Studies
- Nutrition and Exercise Science
- Outdoor Activities
- Outdoor Studies
- Outdoor Studies and Sport
- Physical Activity, Exercise and Health
- Physical Education
- Physical Education and Sport
- Recreation Management
- Sport and Exercise Science
- Sport and Exercise Therapy
- Sport and Fitness Management
- Sport and Leisure
- Sport and Recreation
- Sport Conditioning, Rehabilitation and Coaching
- Sport, Health and Exercise
- Sport, Health and Fitness
- Sports and Leisure Management
- Sports Coaching and Development
- Sports Coaching with Sports Development
- Sports Development
- Sports Development and Physical Education
- Sports Leadership
- Sports Management
- Sports Nutrition
- Sports Psychology
- Sports Technology
- Sports Rehabilitation
- Sports Science
- Sports Science and Injury Management
- Sports Science and Physiology
- Sports Science: Water Sports and Adventure Activities Management
- Sports Studies
- Sports Therapy
- Turf Management.

PART-TIME STUDY

There are plenty of options to gain sport- and fitness-related qualifications while you are in employment. These range from the professional qualifications described on pages 56–9 to HNDs and Foundation degrees.

HEALTH WARNING

When you are looking at different courses always check the content very carefully to make sure it is what you want! There is no requirement for courses with the same title to cover exactly the same topics.

QUESTIONS TO ASK WHEN LOOKING INTO COURSES

- How is this course going to help my career?

- Is it recognised by employers and appropriate professional organisations?

- Can I afford to do it?

- Where do I get the money?

- Could I do the course by part-time study or distance learning?

SOURCES OF INFORMATION

- university and college prospectuses

- university and college websites

- course leaflets

- alternative prospectuses (written by students and pretty realistic!)

- higher education websites – listed at the end of Chapter 4.

BEING PAID TO ENJOY YOUR SPORT

If you play a sport to a high standard (e.g. county level) and are thinking of applying to university, it's worth finding out whether you might be eligible for a sports scholarship.

Quite a number of universities want to attract players of outstanding ability who will represent the university in national competitions. Students receive a bursary (normally between £500 and £1,500), professional coaching workshops, nutritional guidance and sports medicine services. For example:

> **Bath University gives scholarships to 200 of its students in 13 different sports, including athletics, badminton, basketball, bobsleigh, football, hockey, judo, modern pentathlon, netball, rugby, swimming, tennis and triathlon.**
>
> **Exeter University pays students £1,000 a year to help with coaching and training expenses and the cost of travel to competitions and matches. Scholarships are available in athletics, basketball, lacrosse, football, rowing and sports acrobatics.**
>
> **Kent County Cricket Club and the University of Kent provide cricket bursaries to students of high cricketing standard who are willing to play for Kent County Cricket Club.**
>
> **Northumbria University and Newcastle Rugby Football Union offer bursaries to assist students with training and other expenses.**

In all cases, students do the subject of their choice. Many students go on to play sport professionally.

You can find information on sports scholarships in *University Scholarships and Awards*, published by Trotman (see Sources of information).

CASE STUDY

Matt Stevens, Postgraduate student, Cardiff University
Matt has completed a law degree at Cardiff and is now coming towards the end of a postgraduate legal practice course. All through his time at Cardiff he has held a golf bursary.

'I had captained the county under-19 side and played in the Welsh squad before I came to university. Through a friend in the Welsh squad I heard about the bursary system. He told me that I would need a handicap of three or less and would have to be accepted on to a degree course. I could then apply. That is what I did. I chose Cardiff because it is not too far from home and I wanted to go back at weekends to play there.

'Golf scholarships are worth more than those for other sports because the money comes from the Royal and Ancient Golf Club. I get £1,500 to spend on equipment, travel expenses to tournaments and any extra coaching that I think I need. (I have to produce receipts to prove that the money has been spent on golf and not on general student expenses.) Golf is an expensive sport, so I am really pleased to have the bursary.

'The Royal and Ancient want to encourage young golf players who also have academic ambitions to stay in Britain, and if they eventually turn professional, play on the European Circuit rather than go to the USA. If they study there on sports scholarships, it is likely that they will stay in the USA.

'The university provides me with coaching, nutritional advice and help from a sports psychologist. All the sports scholars get dietary advice from the nutritionist who works for the Welsh rugby team. She holds seminars and discussions for us at the university. We also have sessions with a sports psychology lecturer from UWIC (University of Wales College, Cardiff). He specialises in golf and is well known on the European circuit. The seminars are really useful. I always leave them thinking "I learned something today". Eight sessions are allowed each year. If I wanted more I could pay for them from my funding.

'My coach is Rob Butterworth, the Glamorgan and Wales coach.

He is fantastic. In the winter there are not so many tournaments so I see him seven or eight times on a one-to-one basis to keep my game ticking over. We work at the driving range on minor points in my game. Rob videos me hitting balls then plays the tape in slow motion and analyses my shots.

'As far as playing is concerned, I play in the league on Wednesdays and I do go back to play in my home team every Saturday. Other students do the same – and some travel greater distances. I have a friend who goes home to Surrey every Friday evening in order to play at his club there. During my degree course I managed to play three or four times a week but my timetable is heavier this year, so I put in more time at the range in the evenings.

'When I first came to university I had every intention of turning professional when I left. Things change, though – and I am now going to be a solicitor.'

So: there are lots of qualifications, different ways of getting them and different funding methods.

But: courses alone will not get you a job!

THE VALUE OF WORK EXPERIENCE

'Work experience is very important these days. Many employers expect to see it on a CV and some won't look at ones that don't contain details of it. A recent survey showed that it is one of the most successful ways of getting a permanent job. It is important though to start out by deciding just what you want and hope to achieve from a work experience placement – and to work out afterwards what you have gained from it. The time to bring this out is at a job interview when you can describe what you did and what you gained.'

Liz Rhodes, Director of the National Council for
Work Experience

Examples of work experience:

- holiday jobs on children's holiday play schemes

- part-time work as a leisure centre assistant

- part-time work as a lifeguard/pool attendant

- teaching an activity (if you have relevant qualifications) at a residential summer camp

- why not qualify as soon as you can in one leisure activity – aerobics, say – and apply for work at a health club or leisure centre?

You get paid for all these jobs, too.

THE VALUE OF VOLUNTARY WORK

'I cannot stress enough the value of voluntary experience,' says Kevin Harris, a sports development officer. 'I soon found that you don't leave university and just walk into a job! It hit me that I needed a lot more experience and that voluntary work was the way to get it.' To see how he did this and got the job he wanted as a result, see his account on page 38.

Luckily, there are lots and lots of openings for volunteers:

- at events such as youth games

- helping with after-school games and sport in primary schools (or secondary if you are now in higher education)

- in coaching

- on summer sports programmes.

PAYING FOR QUALIFICATIONS

HOW MUCH?

That depends on how old you are and on exactly what you want to do. If, for example, you are 16 and thinking about staying in full-time education for two more years, you shouldn't have to pay very much. Full-time students under 19 normally don't pay tuition fees. (If you want to do a further education course and are over 19, you'll probably be charged a few hundred pounds, but colleges can waive fees for students in financial difficulty.) Do expect, though, to pay for some visits organised as part of the course.

HIGHER EDUCATION

If you are over 18 and planning to go on to higher education – i.e. to a degree or higher diploma course – you might have to make a contribution towards tuition fees, which at present is a maximum sum of £1,150 a year. How much you pay will depend on family income. Some students make the full contribution; others (about 50 per cent) pay nothing. *But* you have probably read of the government's plan to allow universities and colleges to charge variable tuition fees. If Parliament votes this measure through, universities and colleges will be able to charge what they like up to a maximum of £3,000 per year. This change would be introduced from September 2006.

The current situation is different in Scotland from that in the rest of the UK. Scottish students who live in Scotland and attend Scottish universities and colleges pay no tuition fees. They do though, pay a Graduate Endowment – currently £2,000 – when they have qualified and are working.

FINANCIAL HELP

- Students on higher education courses may apply for student loans (maximum £5,050 for students in London and £4,095 elsewhere: 2004–2005 rates). You don't have to pay this back until you have qualified and are earning £15,000 a year. From 2006 it is proposed that students will also pay their tuition fees after they have graduated instead of yearly during the course.

- Grants of up to £1,000 are available for students from lower-income families. These do not have to be paid back.

- If you are likely to be a mature student, there is a whole range of benefits – Lone Parent's Grant, Parents' Learning Allowance and Childcare Grant – that you can claim. Make sure you don't miss any of these! Refer to *Financial Support for Higher Education Students* (see Sources of information).

PROFESSIONAL QUALIFICATIONS
You are on your own here, unfortunately!

You would have to pay for your own training, unless sponsored by an employer, but there are ways of spreading the cost. Most organisations provide courses that can be taken on a part-time basis, which means that you can earn in a in a part-time job – or even full time, if you can juggle your hours – while training.

CAREER DEVELOPMENT LOAN
You could borrow between £300 and £8,000 with the government paying the interest while you are on a full-time course. And you could get grants to cover travel and childcare. You would have to pay the loan back at a fixed rate of interest when the course finished. Career Development Loans are available through Barclays, the Co-operative Bank and the Royal Bank of Scotland. See www.lifelonglearning.co.uk.

SUMMING UP

After all you have read – is a career in sport and fitness for you? Would you like:

● the life style?

● the environment?

● the salary potential?

Remember that all three can vary considerably according to where you are employed and in which area of the country you live.

And don't forget that there are promotion prospects. This is not an industry where entry levels and promotion prospects are rigid. You can get on, but it will be up to you to prove yourself:

● by being good at your job

● by showing that you are willing to learn

● by getting qualified, whether by working for NVQs in your job or taking further courses.

If you really want to get to the top areas of management, it will help to take further academic qualifications. Both Sue Hornibrook and Kevin Harris are doing this (see pp 26–7 and 50–1).

Qualifications are not enough on their own. People who carve out successful careers also have skills. In Chapter 2 we discussed what skills are required to do some of the jobs well. To progress in a career, which invariably means taking on further responsibilities and being in charge of other people and their work, you need in addition to have some general skills. These are also known as transferable skills, because they do not relate to just one career but to many.

What are these transferable skills? See how you rate yourself on these:

● **Communication skills**
  Being able to relate well to people from a wide range of backgrounds, putting your ideas across effectively, explaining to colleagues or junior staff what you want them to do.

● **Commitment**
  Being dependable, punctual, giving a lot to your work.

● **Customer service**
  Keeping customers and clients happy, sorting out any complaints they have, listening to their suggestions.

● **Leadership**
  Taking responsibility and managing other people; getting things done.

● **Problem solving**
  Getting around difficulties, finding a way around problems.

● **Resourcefulness**
Using your initiative, planning ahead, adapting and changing
your plans if you have to do so.

● **Teamworking**
Working well with other people and being able to give and take.

These are the top skills that employers come up with time and
time again when asked which transferable skills they rate most
highly.

A job in sport and fitness does not have to be your first one. There
is plenty of room for career changers. If you are fed up with your
office job, fed up with staring at a computer screen, bored to tears
in your present job – go for it. Ask yourself a few questions first,
though:

● **Am I too old?**
Age isn't too important but your level of fitness (if you want an
active job) is.

● **Can I afford a drop in salary?**
Anyone moving to a new career – in whatever area – is more
than likely to have to take a cut in salary while retraining and
gaining experience. Career changers need to be realistic about
family commitments.

If you're thinking about a full-time course:

● **I haven't done any study for a long time. Will my brain cope?**
Yes. More and more mature students enrol on courses every
year. Interestingly, many more mature students are training in
physiotherapy than used to be the case.

● **Will I get a job at the end of the course?**
No one can predict or give a guarantee, but course tutors
should have a good idea of where past students are working.
So should the college or university careers service. Ask!

CHAPTER 4

Find out more

WHERE TO GET ADVICE

If you are still at school, you should find lots of information in your careers room or library. This should contain many of the books and information from the sources that are recommended in this chapter and under Sources of information. You should also be able to access the Internet at school and look at information in various websites (also recommended). And of course, if you have Internet access at home you can do some research there. If you want advice, talk to your careers teacher and the careers adviser who visits your school. In Northern Ireland, Scotland and Wales, careers advisers work for local careers services. In England they may be known as personal advisers (careers) and will work for the Connexions Service. Careers advisers should be able to point you in the right direction for advice and information. They will also be able to help you decide on the most suitable route and entry point for your career in sports and fitness.

If you are in higher education, make contact with the careers advisory service there. You will find information on different careers in their information rooms; you will be able to use computer programs that link your skills and interests to particular jobs and you will be able to use the graduate careers advisory service system (www.prospects.ac.uk), which contains a wealth of information on careers, training, courses and salaries. You should also be able to book an appointment for an individual guidance session with a careers adviser.

Many higher education careers services also offer:

- information sessions on career areas, e.g. the leisure industry

- job fairs that are visited by employers

- the opportunity to get some relevant work experience

- seminars and workshops on job hunting, CV writing, applications and interviews.

These things really do matter. Apparently graduates – the most highly educated members of the population - often find their applications rejected because they:

- send their CVs and letters to the wrong person (when it takes a few minutes to ring the employer and ask where they should be sent!)

- send letters and CVs that include grammatical and spelling mistakes. (Never rely on your computer's spell-check system. It can come up with some odd ideas. Use an old-fashioned dictionary.)

- turn up to interviews knowing very little about the company. (What's so difficult about logging on to their website?)

Entire books have been written on applying for jobs and on interview technique. There is no need to repeat all the advice here. You can also find advice on the Prospects website, www.prospects.ac.uk, and the Trotman Publishing website, www.trotman.co.uk.

If you are a graduate, you may continue to use the services of your careers advisory service (although some universities and colleges have a cut-off point of a certain number of years after graduation) – and if you no longer live near your old campus, you can try contacting the careers service at your nearest higher education careers service. Many offer help to graduates from other universities and colleges.

Another method is to pay for careers guidance in the private sector. A consultation with such an organisation will probably include psychometric tests followed by discussion and recommendations. Standards of service vary widely, and the service can cost up to £1,000. You can find organisations advertising on the Internet (key 'careers advice' into one of the search engines). You can also complete some tests and questionnaires on the Internet. Why not try these first and see what you think?

The main thing to remember is that there is a lot of information out there and many sources of advice. Make sure that you get as much help as possible.

HOW TO FIND A JOB IN HEALTH AND FITNESS

The press is a good starting point. National newspapers advertise jobs in the public sector on different days of the week. The *Guardian* is good on Wednesdays for jobs in leisure, including recreation management and sports development. Jobs in education are in the *Guardian* on Tuesday, the *Independent* on Thursdays and The *Times Educational Supplement* and *The Times Higher Education Supplement* on Fridays. You will see posts for coaches and sports development officers here as well as for teachers. If you are looking for a job in your own area, try your local newspaper. This should be a good source of junior positions such as leisure centre/sports centre assistant in addition to management jobs.

Professional magazines are another good source. You should be able to find copies in a reference library. Try: *Leisure Management*, *Leisure News and Jobs* (Institute of Leisure and Amenities Management) and *Leisure and Hospitality Business* (Centaur Communications Ltd).

For work in the fitness industry try *Personal Trainer* magazine, which carries advertisements for aerobics instructors, club managers, exercise specialists, fitness instructors, health and fitness managers, massage therapists and personal trainers. Most vacancies are with private-sector organisations, but some local authority jobs are also included.

Noticeboards are worth investigating. Put on your walking shoes, go to the nearest gym, health club, leisure centre and see if any vacancies are advertised.

Many, many jobs are now advertised on the Internet. There are lots of websites for job hunters. Try entering 'sport' and 'jobs' into any of the major search engines – and away you go.

Particularly useful is www.leisureopportunities.co.uk, which advertises a selection of jobs including tennis managers, club managers and assistant managers, fitness instructors, duty officers (in leisure centres), young people's sports and activities co-ordinators, spa managers, gym instructors, reception managers, specialist physical activity officers (mental health), outdoor sport and leisure managers.

Try the websites of any of the professional associations listed under Sources of information below, and also www.jobsgopublic.co.uk, which advertises jobs in sport and leisure on behalf of local authorities.

Don't forget careers services. They may receive job details direct from employers. They will also know of employers you could approach with a speculative application.

PUBLICATIONS

101 Ways to Succeed in Sports Development, ILAM and Leisure Studies Association

Careers 2005, Trotman Publishing – a general careers guide exploring over 700 jobs.

Careers in Sport Compendium, English Sports Council Publications

CRAC Degree Course Guides: Hospitality, Tourism, Leisure and Sport, Trotman Publishing

Degree Course Offers, Brian Heap, Trotman Publishing

Entrance Guide to Higher Education in Scotland, UCAS/Universities Scotland

Financial Support for Higher Education Students, Department for Education and Skills. Free by calling 0800 731 9133 and quoting reference S/FSHE/V4. Also online at www.dfes.gov.uk/studentsupport; or from Student Support Branch, Department for Employment and Learning, Northern Ireland, 028 9025 7710, www.delni.gov.uk/studentsupport; or the Students Awards Agency for Scotland, 0131 476 8212, www.student-support-saas.gov.uk

A Guide to Qualifications in Sport and Recreation, Institute of Leisure and Amenities Management, ILAM

How to Complete Your UCAS Form, Trotman Publishing

Institute of Sport and Recreation Management Information Pack, Institute of Sport and Recreation Management

National Coaching Federation – Careers in Sport, Sports Coach UK

National Coaching Federation – Outdoor Pursuits and National Sports Centres, Sports Coach UK
National Coaching Federation – Sources of Information, Sports Coach UK
National Coaching Federation – Sports Governing Bodies, Sports Coach UK
Sports Information Leaflet No.1 – General Information, Sport Scotland
Student Book 2005, Trotman Publishing
UCAS Directory – for a list of higher education courses
University and College Entrance: The Official Guide, UCAS
University Scholarships and Awards, Brian Heap, Trotman Publishing

MAGAZINES

Leisure Management, The Leisure Media Company Ltd
Leisure News and Jobs, Institute of Leisure and Amenities Management
Leisure and Hospitality Business, Centaur Communications Ltd
Personal Trainer, Premier Training and Development

ORGANISATIONS

British Association of Sport and Exercise Sciences
114 Cardigan Road
Headingley
Leeds LS6 3BJ
0113 289 1020
www.bases.org.uk

British Olympic Association
1 Wandsworth Plain
London SW18 1EH
Tel: 020 8871 2677
www.olympics.org.uk

British Paralympic Association
BPA, Norwich Union Building
9th Floor
69 Park Lane
Croydon CR9 1BG
Tel: 020 7662 888
www.paralympics.org.uk

England and Wales Cricket Board
Lords Cricket Ground
London NW8 8QZ
020 7432 1200
www.ecb.co.uk

Football Association
25 Soho Square
London W1D 4FA
020 7745 4545
www.the-fa.org

Footballers' Further Education and Vocational Training Society Ltd.
2 Oxford Court
Bishopsgate
Manchester M2 3WO

Institute of Groundsmanship
19–23 Church Street
Wolverton
Milton Keynes
Bucks MK12 5LG
01908 312511
www.iog.org.uk

Institute of Leisure and Amenity Management
ILAM House
Lower Basildon
Reading
Berks RG8 9NE
01491 874800
www.ilam.co.uk

Institute of Professional Sport
Francis House
Francis Street
London SW1P 1DE
020 7854 8500

Institute of Sport and Recreational Management
Giffard House
36–38 Sherrard Street
Melton Mowbray
Leicestershire LE13 1XJ
01664 565531
www.isrm.co.uk

Keep Fit Association
Astra House, Suite 105
Arklow Road
London SE14 6EB
020 88692 9566
www.keepfit.org.uk

Lawn Tennis Association
The Queen's Club
Barons Court
Palliser Road
West Kensington
London W14 9EG
020 7381 7000
www.lta.org.uk

Mountain Leader Training Board
177 Burton Road
West Didsbury
Manchester M20 2BB
0161 445 4747
www.mltb.org

National Register of Personal Trainers
254–258 Belsize Road
London NW6 4BT
0870 200 6010
www.nrpt.co.uk

National Sports Medicine Institute of the United Kingdom
32 Devonshire Street London
W1G 6PX
020 7251 0583

www.nsmi.org.uk
The Register of Exercise and Sports Care at the above address
has the following website: www.rescu.org.uk

Physical Education Association of the UK
Building 25
London Road
Reading
Berks. RG1 5AQ
0118 931 6240
www.pea.uk.com

Premier Training and Development Ltd.
Parade House
70 Fore Street
Trowbridge
Wiltshire
BA14 8HQ
01225 353574

Professional Golfers' Association
Centenary House
The Belfry
Sutton Coldfield
West Midlands B76 9PT
01675 470333
www.pga.org.uk

Sport England
3rd Floor, Victoria House
Bloomsbury
London WC1B 4SE
020 7273 1500
www.sportengland.org

Skillsactive (Sports and Recreation Industry Training Organisation)
24 Stephenson Way
London NW1 2HD
020 7388 7755
www.skillsactive.com

Sports Coach UK (National Coaching Federation)
114 Cardigan Road
Headingley
Leeds LS6 3BJ
0113 274 4802
www.ncf.org.uk

Sports Council for Northern Ireland
House of Sport
Upper Malone Road
Belfast BT9 5LA
028 9038 1222
www.sportni.org

Sports Council for Wales
Information Centre, Welsh Institute of Sport
Sophia Gardens
Cardiff CF11 9SW
029 2030 0500
www.sports-council-wales.co.uk

Sports Scotland
Caledonia House
1 Redheughs Rigg
South Gyle
Edinburgh EH12 9DQ
0131 317 7200
www.sportscotland.org.uk

UK Sport (UK Sports Council)
40 Bernard Street
London WC1N 1ST
020 7211 5246
www.uksport.gov.uk

Universities and Colleges Admissions Service (UCAS)
Rosehill
New Barn Lane
Cheltenham
Gloucestershire GL52 3LZ
01242 227788
www.ucas.com

YMCA Fitness Industry Training
111, Great Russell Street
London WC1B 3NP
020 7343 1850
info@ymcafit.org.ukrn

OTHER WEBSITES

www.jobsgopublic.co.uk
www.leisureopportunities.co.uk
www.lifelonglearning.co.uk and www.support4learning.org.uk – for
more information on financing study
www.monster.co.uk
www.occupationsonline.gov.uk
www.prospects.ac.uk – a careers site for students in higher
education
www.trotman.co.uk
www.workthing.co.uk